1,234
QUITE
INTERESTING
FACTS

TO LEAVE YOU SPEECHLESS

1,234 QUITE INTERESTING FACTS

TO LEAVE YOU SPEECHLESS

Compiled by
John Lloyd, John Mitchinson,
and James Harkin

with the QI Elves
Anne Miller, Andrew Hunter Murray,
Anna Ptaszynski, Dan Schreiber,
and Alex Bell

W. W. Norton & Company
Independent Publishers Since 1923
New York | London

For information about permission to reproduce selections from this book,
write to Permissions, W. W. Norton & Company, Inc., 500 Fifth Avenue,
New York, NY 10110

For information about special discounts for bulk purchases, please contact
W. W. Norton Special Sales at specialsales@wwnorton.com or 800-233-4830

Manufacturing by RR Donnelley Harrisonburg
Production manager: Julia Druskin

Library of Congress Cataloging-in-Publication Data
Names: Lloyd, John, 1951– author. | Mitchinson, John, 1963– co-author. |
Harkin, James, 1971– co-author.
Title: 1,234 quite interesting facts to leave you speechless / compiled by John
Lloyd, John Mitchinson, and James Harkin.
Other titles: One thousand two hundred thirty-four quite interesting facts to
leave you speechless | Twelve hundred thirty-four quite interesting facts to
leave you speechless
Description: New York : W.W. Norton & Company, 2016. | Includes
bibliographical references and index.
Identifiers: LCCN 2016019970 | ISBN 9780393254488 (hardcover)
Subjects: LCSH: Curiosities and wonders. | Handbooks, vade-mecums, etc. |
History—Miscellanea. | Science—Miscellanea.
Classification: LCC AG243 .L565 2016 | DDC 031.02--dc23 LC record
available at https://lccn.loc.gov/2016019970

W. W. Norton & Company, Inc.
500 Fifth Avenue, New York, N.Y. 10110
www.wwnorton.com

W. W. Norton & Company Ltd.
15 Carlisle Street, London W1D 3BS

1 2 3 4 5 6 7 8 9 0

Contents

[v]

Introduction

The world is made up of facts, not things.
LUDWIG WITTGENSTEIN

The word "fact" has a curious history.

When it first appeared in English in the early 15th century, it had a quite different meaning from the one we use today. It came from the Latin *facere*, "to do or make," and meant "something done"—a "deed" or "act." And, for the first hundred years of its existence, it carried mostly negative connotations.

As "silly" once meant "holy" and "bully" meant "sweetheart," "facts" weren't so much true as bad. The world, the truth, and particularly the language is in flux everywhere. Today, we use "fact" as a signifier of truth—something that has actually occurred—but, as keen viewers of *QI* will know, even the best facts often don't last forever.

A hundred years from now, the fact that a soccer player is three times more likely to be bitten by Luis Suárez than by a snake will be meaningless, and no one will care that in 2014, more American babies were named Khaleesi than Adele.

On the other hand, it's likely that bees will continue to have five eyes.

And you still won't be able to hum and whistle at the same time.

For us, facts like these are the currency of wonder, the small change that opens the turnstile between the everyday world and the wild and mysterious universe beyond.

Fare forward, traveler—and wrap up

well! The wind coming from the center of
the Milky Way is traveling at two million
mph . . .

JOHN LLOYD, JOHN MITCHINSON,

AND JAMES HARKIN

A fact is an Epiphany of God and on every fact of his life man should rear a temple of wonder and joy.

RALPH WALDO EMERSON (1803–1882)

1,234
QUITE
INTERESTING
FACTS

TO LEAVE YOU SPEECHLESS

The Big Bang
was quieter than
a Motörhead concert.

The astronomer
who coined the term
"Big Bang" didn't
believe in it.

The scientist who
analyzed the plutonium for
the first atomic bomb was
called Mr. Doom.

The president of the
World Chess Federation
believes that, unless we play
more chess, the world
will be destroyed
by aliens.

The world champion
of French Scrabble
doesn't speak
French.

There are 19 languages
on Earth with only
one speaker left.

There are
at least 17 types of ice,
but only one exists outside
the laboratory.

Firefighters
add a "wetting agent" to
make their water
even wetter.

It takes 50 glasses of water
to grow the oranges to make
one glass of orange juice.

Orange skin
caused by eating
too many carrots is called
carotenemia.

If you plant an apple seed,
the new tree will bear apples
that are completely different from
the one the seed came from.

Some mushrooms
have 28,000
sexes.

Magic mushrooms
grow in the gardens of
Buckingham Palace.

When the Queen gave
birth to Prince Charles,
Prince Philip was
playing squash.

Table tennis was
banned in the USSR
from 1930 to 1950 on
the grounds that it
was harmful to
people's eyes.

Wearing white at
Wimbledon began as a
way of hiding the fact
that women sweat.

The British men
most likely to wear
pink boxer shorts
live in London.

The average
British nurse eats
six free chocolates a day.

The "Radio Nurse"
was the first baby monitor.
It came with a matching transmitter
called the "Guardian Ear."

The founder
of the *Daily Mail* was
convinced that Belgians
were poisoning his
ice cream.

In 19th-century London,
fake ice cream was made from
mashed turnip.

In 2014,
a Birmingham woman
called 911 because her
ice cream didn't have enough
sprinkles on it.

To test what happens if
someone sits on their phone,
Samsung has a robot
shaped like a
bottom.

Between 2003 and 2015,
9,000 Americans lost fingers
in snowblower
accidents.

Two-thirds of all the
people killed by volcanoes
lived in Indonesia.

Most Indonesians
speak Indonesian as a
second language.

Kim Jong-un is the
only person in North Korea
called Kim Jong-un.

The pseudonyms of
Benjamin Franklin included
Silence Dogood, Anthony Afterwit,
Alice Addertongue, Harry Meanwell,
Martha Careful, Busy Body,
and Richard Saunders.

The four most
common first names among
New York City taxi drivers are
Mohammad, Mohammed,
Muhammad, and Mohamed.

Not a single car
was sold by Buzz Aldrin
in the six months he worked as
a car salesman on his return
from the Moon.

Neil Armstrong
once sued his barber
for selling a lock
of his hair.

In May 2014,
the Moon had faster broadband
than Maine, Kentucky, and Montana.

More people work for
the Chinese government
monitoring the Internet
than serve in its
armed forces.

There are four million
songs on Spotify that have
never been played.

In 2009,
92% of songs
in the *Billboard* Top 100 had
"reproductive themes."

At any given time,
50% of "sexters" are lying
about what they
are doing.

On average, people are
two inches shorter and
20% poorer than they
claim to be online.

Half of your anecdotes
are stolen from
someone else.

A blue whale can
swallow half a million calories
in a single mouthful.

The world champion jockey
Laffit Pincay Jr.
kept his weight down by
eating half a peanut for lunch.

In 1923,
jockey Frank Hayes
won a race despite being
dead.

In 1937
at Romford dog track
you could watch cheetah racing.

Kaiser Wilhelm II
loved riding so much he
sat at his desk astride a saddle.
He said it helped him
think more clearly.

Sir Walter Scott's
salt cellar was made from
a neck bone belonging to
King Charles I.

Albert Einstein's eyeballs
are in a safety deposit box
in New York.

A newborn baby can't see
the expression on your face
if you're more than
12 inches away.

Blue whales
don't know they're blue.
They can only see in
black and white.

Composer Erik Satie
only ate white food.

@

For 42,000 years,
humans used cow's milk
to paint with before
anyone thought
to drink it.

A glass of cow's milk
has twice as much solid content
as a tomato.

Female kangaroos can
produce whole and skim milk
simultaneously.

Dolphin's milk
is as thick as
toothpaste.

Chalk
is made from
algae.

Birmingham University
sits on top of a mile
of fake coal mine.

The M96 is
a fake highway
used for firefighting
practice.

The world's first road
built exclusively for cars
is now a bicycle path.

In the late 19th century,
women cyclists were warned
they might get "bicycle face,"
giving them a jutting chin
and bulging eyes.

In 1849,
"running amok"
was an officially recognized
medical condition.

In 1495,
the Spanish mixed
lepers' blood with wine
to give to the French.

In the 16th century,
it was thought that
sitting in cow dung
cured diarrhea.

The first-ever
fire engine was called
the "Sucking Worm."

In 1900,
Sir Arthur Conan Doyle caught fire
during a cricket match at Lord's.
The ball hit a box of matches
in his pocket.

In 2011,
two Iranian soccer players
were suspended for celebratory
bottom-patting.

In 2010,
Iran banned
mullet haircuts.

The Danish for "mullet"
is *Bundesligahår*, meaning
"the hair of a German
soccer player."

Until 1912,
soccer goalkeepers were allowed
to handle the ball anywhere
in their own half.

Until 1882,
baseball umpires could
confer with the crowd if
they weren't sure whether
a catch had been made.

The first mini golf course
was invented for women who
weren't allowed to
play real golf.

①

In his 27-year reign,
Pope John Paul II took
more than 100 skiing and
mountain-climbing holidays.

The Pope
is not allowed to be
an organ donor because his body
"belongs to the whole Church."

No one
in the UK
dies of natural causes.

Baths
kill more people
than terrorists do.

Americans
wash their hands
800 billion times a year.

Newborn Spartan boys
were immediately
washed in wine.

Newborn babies can
recognize the theme song from
their mother's favorite
soap opera.

Alex Salmond,
former first minister of Scotland,
once appeared in
a Bollywood soap opera.

An India versus Pakistan
cricket match in 2015
was watched by more
than a billion people.

The winning goal in the
first-ever World Cup final
was scored by a
one-armed man.

Neanderthals
took care of their
old and disabled.

Early humans
first caught bedbugs
from sharing caves
with bats.

During the Second World War,
15,000 people lived in
caves in Kent.

15,000 years ago,
cannibalism was practiced
in the UK.

The world's first powered flight
took place in Chard,
Somerset, in 1848.

The Wright brothers
flew together only once.
Their father forbade it
in case they crashed.

Immediately after
the Wright brothers' first flight,
a gust of wind flipped their plane over
and broke it.

The wind coming from
the center of the Milky Way
is traveling at two million mph.

At 60 mph,
most of the noise a car makes
comes from contact with the road,
not from the engine.

At the oldest known
drive-through you could
order bullets.

The bullet was invented
thousands of years before
the gun.

Paintings of a
15,000-year-old bison
were accidentally erased in 1992
by a group of French youths
removing graffiti
from a cave.

Medical error
is the third-largest killer of
patients in US hospitals.

Newspapers
correct fewer than 2%
of their mistakes.

Until 1922, you could listen to
the news by telephone.

The oldest person in history was
born the year Alexander Graham Bell
made the first sound transmission
and died the year that Puff Daddy
had his US No. 1 hit
"I'll Be Missing You."

The world's oldest land animal is a
183-year-old giant tortoise named Jonathan.
He was born in the same year as
Louisa May Alcott.

In 2008,
the National Toy Hall of Fame
gave its "Oldest Toy" award
to the stick.

The ancient Greeks
played with
yo-yos.

Twister
was originally called
"King's Footsie."

The Chinese for
shuffling mah-jongg tiles
translates as the
"twittering of the sparrows."

Verbs in the Archi language
of southern Russia can take
1,502,839 possible forms.

Ⓘ

In 2001,
Saudi Arabia
banned Pokémon
for "promoting Zionism."

Saudi Arabia
imports camels
from Australia.

Building on sand
illegally exported from
Malaysia and Indonesia,
Singapore has expanded by
20% since the 1960s.

Since the 1930s,
American turkeys
have more than
doubled in size.

When male turkeys
see female turkeys,
they blush.

In the Middle Ages,
strapping a live chicken
to the body was thought
to cure plague.

Soldiers in Iraq
deployed live chickens to warn
of possible chemical attacks.
This was known as "Operation
Kuwaiti Field Chicken (KFC)."

The last McDonald's burger
in Iceland was sold in 2009,
but it can still be watched
decomposing on a webcam.

The Icelandic word
for "pager" translates as
"thief of the peace."

The Icelandic word
for "computer" translates as
"number prophetess."

Arthur Scherbius,
inventor of the Enigma machine,
also invented an
electric pillow.

The first search engine was
called Archie and was built in 1989
by a man who hasn't owned
a computer since 1983.

In 2010,
the US military
built a supercomputer
out of 1,760 PlayStation 3s.

After winning
the US quiz show *Jeopardy*,
the IBM supercomputer "Watson"
went back to work in health care.

Mary Shelley kept
Percy Shelley's heart
wrapped in a poem for
30 years after his death.

In 2008,
the 18th-century German poet
Friedrich Schiller was sent
two reminders to pay
his TV bill.

Abraham Lincoln
was a licensed bartender.

Rod Stewart lost his job as
a wallpaper designer
because he was
color-blind.

Vladimir Putin's grandfather
worked as a chef for
Stalin and Lenin,
and Rasputin.

Oliver Twist was modeled on
Butch Cassidy's grandfather.

Davros from *Doctor Who*
and Professor Yaffle from *Bagpuss*
were both based on the philosopher
Bertrand Russell.

The translation of
Harry Potter and the Philosopher's Stone
into ancient Greek is the longest
ancient Greek text produced
since AD 3.

The doctor who
administered enemas to
ancient Egyptian pharaohs was
called the "shepherd of the royal anus."

Box jellyfish
have 64 anuses.

Ⓠ

Battery hens
were invented by
the ancient Romans.

In ancient Sumeria,
the laws of civilization
and the universe were
called "meh."

It's against the law
in the US to own
golden eagle
feathers.

In 2014,
a man in the Italian town of Bra
was arrested for
stealing bras.

In Thailand,
the National Office of Buddhism
has a hotline for complaints
about unruly monks.

The blast furnace, the @ sign,
pretzels, and genetics were
all invented by monks.

In the 15th century,
a biting epidemic swept through
the nunneries of Germany,
Holland, and Rome.

Gorillas are vegetarians
but their bite is
twice as powerful
as a lion's.

Frankenstein's monster
was a vegetarian.

84% of American vegetarians
will end up eating meat.

Finnish budget meatballs
have so little meat in them
they have had to be
renamed
"balls."

The average supermarket
contains enough food to
keep you alive for 55 years,
or 63 years if you don't mind
eating pet food.

At least
18 species of spider
catch and eat
fish.

The world's largest spider
weighs as much as
seven bags of
chips.

Filmgoers
eat *55%* more popcorn
watching a sad film
than a comedy.

In Chile,
popcorn is called
cabritas, or "little goats,"
because of the way it
jumps in the pan.

One billion chicken wings,
five million pounds of pretzels, and
four million pounds of popcorn are
eaten on Super Bowl Sunday.

Guantánamo Bay
has a gift shop.

Almost half of American adults
think that dinosaurs and
humans coexisted.

There is one
divorce in the US
every 36 seconds.

People are more likely to
believe in global warming if
you ask them in a room
containing a dead plant.

Talking to someone while
holding a warm cup of coffee
makes you more likely to think
of them as a warm person.

You're more likely to
catch a cold by holding hands
with someone than by
kissing them.

When women ovulate,
their faces get slightly
redder, but men
don't notice.

According to Fijian tradition,
the larger a woman's hair,
the more beautiful she is.

After the Chinese Manchu dynasty
conquered the Han people,
they made all the males
wear pigtails.

The average American woman
spends more than $10,000
on shaving products
in her lifetime.

Glowworms
are female fireflies.

A female butterfly
has a second stomach
attached to her vagina.

The horn of the dung beetle
Onthophagus raffrayi
is more than twice the
length of its body.

A colossal squid
swallows through
its brain.

The movements
of octopuses have
no rhythm.

When people sing
together in a choir,
their heartbeats
synchronize.

The man with
the world's deepest voice
can make sounds that only
elephants can hear.

The worse a male
ring-tailed lemur smells,
the more offspring
he will have.

Male scorpion flies
use their penises to
swat away spiders.

More than
300 species of spider
pretend to be ants.

Agatha Christie was
still speaking to imaginary friends
well into her seventies.

Danish people
rate Santa Claus as more friendly
and more reliable than
most doctors.

Kurt Cobain
addressed his suicide note
to his imaginary friend,
Boddah.

Kurt Cobain's
first band was called
Fecal Matter.

The feces of Americans
are a much less diverse ecosystem
for bacteria than those of
Papua New Guineans.

There are more bacteria on Earth
than there are stars in the
known universe.

There are more bacteria
in your armpit than there are
people in the world.

Dogs can
smell floating whale poo
from a mile away.

Camels can
open and close
their nostrils.

Astronauts' eyes
get flatter in space.

Bees
have five eyes.

Mumps
is five times
as contagious as
Ebola.

5% of
Ethiopian
epauletted fruit bats
have the Ebola virus.

In the US in 2014,
there were ten times
as many cases of measles as
there were for the entire
decade 2001–10.

A third of
all the computers in the world
contain at least
one virus.

Uzbekistan shuts down the Internet
during the nation's standardized
annual university entrance exam,
and disables all text messaging.

In the 1850s,
the entrance exam for the Royal Navy
involved writing out the Lord's Prayer
and jumping over a chair naked.

In 1853,
the *Venus de Milo* was
put on trial for nudity
in Germany.

In 2012,
a law banning nudity
in San Francisco was proposed
by a politician called
Scott Wiener.

From 1784 to 1830,
the member of Parliament
for Devon, UK, was called
John Bastard.

The world's biggest drilling machine
is called Bertha.

The 192nd
most powerful supercomputer
in the world is
called Gordon.

There are 299 places in Iran
called Mohammadabad.

There are craters on Mars
called Bristol, Corby, Crewe,
Tooting, and Woking.

Mars is
more accurately mapped
than Alaska.

Thanks to the US military,
the most accurately mapped
country in the world
is Afghanistan.

In 2010,
the British Army parachuted
spy dogs into Afghanistan
to flush out insurgents.

The first cow to
fly in an airplane was
Elm Farm Ollie in 1930.
Her handler milked her and
parachuted cartons of milk
down to spectators below.

D. H. Lawrence
had a cow called Susan.

Cows
have only bottom teeth.

Cows make friends
and get sad when they are
separated from them.

1 in 10 Britons
say they have
no close friends.

Most Britons
tell 10 lies a week.

A third of Britons
say they neither
"love" nor "hate"
Marmite.

The British have
the best teeth of
any Western country.

Every team in
North America's
National Ice Hockey League
has a team dentist.

Between 2003 and 2008,
the lost and found office of
Madame Tussauds collected
123 pairs of false teeth
and one false leg.

97% of the world's tigers
have been lost over
the past century.

Kaiser Wilhelm II
lost a valuable arms contract
by slapping the king of Bulgaria
on the bottom.

The word "sovereign"
is from the Latin *superanus*,
meaning "highest one."

The first-ever children's picture book
was in Latin and had instructions
for beer brewing and
winemaking.

The largest book
ever printed was
The Little Prince.

The Very Hungry Caterpillar
was originally called
A Week with Willi the Worm.

Ian Fleming
said "James Bond" was
the dullest name he'd
ever heard.

Boris Karloff changed his name
from William Henry Pratt
to save embarrassing
his family.

Two-thirds of actors
in the Screen Actors Guild
earn less than $1,000 a year.

Speeding fines in Finland
reflect the offender's earnings.
In 2002, a Nokia executive doing
46 mph in a 31 mph zone was
fined $175,000.

More people in the world
have mobile phones than
have flush toilets.

Harpo Marx
kept a harp in his bathroom
so he could practice while
on the toilet.

"Jingle Bells" was
the first song played
in space.

9 out of 10
artificial Christmas trees
are made in China.

The average Father Christmas
on Christmas cards appears to be
28 pounds lighter than he was
10 years ago.

The first
commercial Christmas card
featured a drawing of a toddler
drinking a glass of wine.

In 2014,
a brewer from Virginia made a
beer from 35-million-year-old yeast.
It was described as tasting
"Belgian."

French fries
were invented
in Belgium.

In Japan,
McDonald's is pronounced
makudonarudo.

There is a city in Japan
called Obama.

In Japan,
bushusuru ("to Bush") means "to vomit"
after George Bush Sr. vomited in
the Japanese PM's lap in 1992.

Japan
is home to
5.52 million vending machines.

The Infantograph,
a machine that predicts
what a couple's baby will look like,
was invented by Dr. Seuss.

Irresistibubble,
the tagline for Aero,
was coined by Salman Rushdie.

Before he invented television,
John Logie Baird invented
the Baird Undersock to
combat trench foot.

Glitter was
invented by accident
by a cattle rancher from
New Jersey.

Manet's son Léon
may in fact have been his half-brother
because his wife Suzanne had
an affair with his father.

Francis and Mary Huntrodd were
both born on September 19, 1600.
They got married on their birthday
and died on September 19, 1680,
within five hours of each other.

Leonard "Live Forever" Jones
was an American politician who
claimed he'd achieved immortality
through clean living.
He died in 1868, aged 71.

No US president
has ever died
in May.

There are more porn sites
hosted in the US
than there are people
in the US.

There are more people on
America's "suspected terrorist" list
than live in the whole
of Estonia.

Americans eat
350 slices of pizza
every second.

The atmosphere of Venus
is so hot it would cook a
pizza in seven seconds.

In 2013,
after six months monitoring
two suspected Chinese spy drones
invading their airspace, the
Indian army discovered
they were Jupiter
and Venus.

In Florida in 2012,
a woman called Crystal Methany
was arrested for drug possession.

In 2011, the Chinese military
tried to pass off a scene from *Top Gun*
as footage of its own air force.

In 2010,
a doctor in Blackpool spent $1,800
trying to win a giant cuddly toy
at a ringtoss stall.

The all-time fastest-selling
Playmobil figure, issued in 2015,
is Martin Luther, complete with
quill pen and German Bible.

Pixar
accidentally deleted *Toy Story 2*
halfway through making it.

In the 1940s,
many stores refused to stock
Mr. Potato Head as it encouraged
children to play with their food
during rationing.

The US has an
awards ceremony called
Potato Man of the Year.

Most US pop songs
are written for people
with a reading age of nine.

Keira Knightley's
first name is a spelling mistake
by her mother.

The real name
of the rapper Akon
is Aliaune Damala Bouga Time
Bongo Puru Nacka Lu Lu Lu
Badara Akon Thiam.

"Waterloo Sunset," by the Kinks,
was originally called
"Liverpool Sunset."

The world's oldest
footprints outside Africa
were found on a beach
in Norfolk.

The world's oldest spiderweb
was found in amber in
East Sussex.

The world's most complete
fossil of a *Tyrannosaurus rex*
has its teeth wrapped round
the most complete fossil
of a triceratops.

When the dinosaurs were alive,
there were active volcanoes
on the Moon.

A restaurant in Lanzarote
cooks its food using the heat
from a volcano.

The Shredded Wheat company
once had a restaurant offering
Shredded Wheat ice cream
and roast turkey served with
Shredded Wheat stuffing.

The Tlatelcomila cannibals
of ancient Mexico ate human flesh
with chili sauce.

The American criminal
known as "the Swiss Cheese Pervert"
for having sex covered in cheese
is from Philadelphia.

Uncle Ben's rice
was invented in Britain
by a German chemist.

Ninjas sent
secret messages using
colored grains of rice.

British war censors
found James Joyce's book *Ulysses*
so difficult to read that they
were convinced it was
written in code.

The world's most successful hacker
was himself hacked and arrested
because his password was
his cat's name
plus "123."

The underwater cable
that powers the Internet
in Southeast Asia is
being eaten by sharks.

1 in 6 dolphins
in the Bahamas have been
bitten by a shark.

The word
"Godzilla" means
"Gorilla-Whale."

A crayfish can
grow new brain cells
from its blood cells.

Penguins
can't taste fish.

Catfish
hunt pigeons.

Owls
sunbathe.

Dolphins
can't sneeze.

Because there are
10 billion trillion nematode worms,
the vast majority of animals
don't have legs.

The oldest known
snake fossil had
four feet.

Some male spiders have
special legs designed to hold
females' jaws open during sex
so they don't get eaten.

Carib cannibals
slit the legs of their victims
and ate them stuffed
with pimentos.

Before the
invention of anesthesia,
amputating a leg took
under a minute.

Smokers are
16 times more likely to
have a limb amputated
than nonsmokers.

Pez dispensers are
shaped like cigarette lighters
because they were designed
to help stop smoking.

Four of the six
"Marlboro men" have died
of smoking-related
diseases.

In 2015,
Italy sent the
first espresso machine
into space.

10% of all the food
stolen in Italy in 2006
was Parmesan.

1.5 million shopping carts are
stolen from British supermarkets
every year.

If Walmart's workforce
were an army, it would be
the second largest
in the world.

The 65 square miles
of northern France that are
still uninhabitable after the
First World War will take
300 years to make safe.

In the last 500 years,
a third of the floods in the
southern Netherlands were created
by humans as weapons of war.

All the American war dead
on European soil were buried
facing away from Germany,
apart from George S. Patton,
who is facing his troops.

Every hour,
one US war veteran
commits suicide.

In the month after
Marilyn Monroe died,
there was a 12% jump in
the US suicide rate.

At least 1 in 10 people
in the Stone Age were murdered,
compared to 1 in 100,000 today.

Neanderthals
hunted and ate
pigeons.

Bhutan has
an official yeti hunter.
He hasn't found any
(at least, not yeti).

In the early 2000s,
Tonga's finance minister
was also its official
court jester.

The *copreae* were
jesters in the Roman imperial court.
Their name translates as
the "little shits."

Roman slaves
had their foreheads
tattooed with the words
"Stop me, I'm a runaway."

There are more tattoos on
British teachers than there are
on members of the British
armed services.

Henry III of France
loved the game of cup-and-ball
so much he set up schools to
teach people how to play.

Jack Nicholson
once got detention at school
every single day for a year.

US chess grandmaster
Bobby Fischer went to school
with Barbra Streisand.
She had a crush on him.

According to North Korea's
official teachers' manual,
Kim Jong-un learned to drive
at the age of three.

In 2000,
Ushers brewery in Trowbridge
was dismantled and rebuilt
in a cabbage patch
in North Korea.

In the 1930s,
England had 3,000
dedicated ginger beer
breweries.

In 1710,
the boys of Winchester College
rioted over inadequate
beer rations.

The state treasurer
of Alabama is called
Young Boozer.

The largest
poster ever produced
features the president and
prime minister of Turkey
and is two-thirds the size
of a soccer field.

US President James Garfield's
favorite meal was
squirrel soup.

Teddy bears
are named after President
Theodore "Teddy" Roosevelt.

Teddy Roosevelt's sons
Theodore and Kermit
were the first Westerners to
shoot a giant panda.

A sniper
was originally someone who
shot snipe.

Merry-go-rounds
were originally a training device
for knights.

The word "aquarium"
originally meant "a watering place
for cattle."

One of the names
originally proposed for Neanderthals
was *Homo stupidus.*

Humans
have shorter attention spans
than goldfish.

The average woman
deletes four selfies for
every one she's happy with.

The only person
ever killed by a boa constrictor
was an escapologist who got
into a coffin with one.

There are
six billion kinds
of knots.

The only meteorite
known to have hit a person
is called the "Hodges Meteorite":
it slightly injured Mrs. Ann Hodges
in Alabama in 1954.

Isaac Newton
walked out of the
only opera he ever attended.

Alan Shepard,
the only man to
play golf on the Moon,
missed the ball on his
first attempt.

The UK's Ministry of Defence
owns 15 golf courses.

The US government
spends $300,000 a year
studying the body language of
other countries' leaders.

The British government
in the 1830s spent $25,000
developing a working model
of Charles Babbage's computer –
more than twice the cost of
a warship at the time.

In 1910,
France had more airplanes than
Germany, Britain, Italy, Russia, Japan,
and the US combined.

The front between Islamic State and
the Iraqi Kurds in 2015 was 50%
longer than the Western Front in 1914.

The US military is America's
largest purchaser of explosives;
number two is Disney World.

After Disney released
The Princess and the Frog,
more than 50 children were
hospitalized with salmonella
after trying to kiss frogs.

Walt Disney
used to pack his testicles in ice
to help improve his
sperm count.

96% of sperm cells
are abnormal.

A whale's sperm cell is
about the same size
as a human one.

Starfish
breathe and smell
through their
feet.

Sniffer dogs
can be trained to find
USB drives.

Bats' throats
contain the fastest muscles
of any mammal.

After fights,
Roman gladiators
drank vinegar mixed with ash
to help their bodies recover.

Gladiators prepared for combat
by covering themselves
with marshmallow sap.

The movie *Gladiator*
used up the entire supply
of plaster on
Malta.

The first pornographic movie
came out in 1895, a few months after
the first regular movie.

The Big Parade (1925) was the
first film to include a swear word.
As it was a silent movie,
the word "damn" appeared
on a dialogue card.

In *The Exorcist*,
the sound effect of the girl's neck
ratcheting round was made by
the director twisting his
cracked leather wallet.

Airplane! was released in Germany
as *The Unbelievable Journey
in a Crazy Airplane*.

The Italian for "break a leg" is
"*in culo alla balena!*"—literally
"into the arse of a whale!"

The Arabic for "incubator"
literally translates as
"chicken machine."

When *Fawlty Towers*
was broadcast in Spain,
Manuel became an Italian
named Paolo.

The Roman poet Catullus
claimed the Spanish used their
morning urine as
a mouthwash.

In 2015,
Islamic State threatened 80 lashes
for anyone caught watching
Real Madrid play Barcelona.

The first version of
soccer's offside rule stated that
players shouldn't "loiter"
near the opposing goal.

In a game of soccer in 1280,
a player was killed after running
into another player's dagger.

Before they got whistles,
football referees waved
a handkerchief.

FIFA
has 18 more members
than the UN.

Until the FA banned
women's soccer in 1921,
it was more popular
than men's.

There are fewer women
on corporate boards in America
than there are men
named John.

If your parents
are happily married,
your risk of divorce
decreases
by 14%.

Under medieval Welsh law
women could divorce their
husbands if they had
bad breath.

On the streets of Mumbai,
you can get your ears
cleaned for
38 cents
an ear.

When the telephone was invented,
there were concerns it would create
left-eared people.

In 1969,
to protect them from noise
elephants living near Heathrow
were given earmuffs.

An elephant's sense of smell
is so good it can distinguish
between members of different
African tribes.

Dogs
investigate bad smells
with their right nostril and
good smells with their left.

The Navajo name for
Adolf Hitler translates as
"he who smells his mustache."

Titan,
Saturn's largest moon,
smells like a mixture of
gasoline and farts.

Moles
smell in stereo.

Moles
have two thumbs
on each hand.

Moles can dig
at a rate equivalent to a man
shifting 3,000 shovel-loads
of earth an hour.

Mankind has reached
20 billion miles beyond the Earth
but only seven and a half
miles inside it.

A gram of soil
contains a million
different species.

Luke Skywalker's lightsaber
from *Return of the Jedi* spent
two weeks in space on the
shuttle *Discovery* in 2007.

The International Space Station is
the single most expensive
object ever built.

Three-quarters of astronauts
take sleeping pills.

South Korea shut down
its entire space program in 2014
when its only astronaut
resigned.

The word "bull" means
"lightbulb" in North Korea and
"testicle" in South Korea.

At their current birth rate,
there will be no South Koreans
at all by 2750.

The rate of extinction for species in
the 20th century was 100 times higher
than it would have been
without human impact.

The iceberg that hit the *Titanic*
was 3,000 years old; it formed when
Tutankhamun was pharaoh.

Tutankhamun
was the owner of all
the ancient Egyptian socks
that have survived.

The only carnivorous mouse
in North America
eats scorpions and
howls at the Moon.

Sanskrit has 40 words for "mouse,"
including "*mushka*," which means
both "little mouse"
and "testicle."

Agatha Christie gave
the rights to *The Mousetrap*
to her grandson as a
birthday present.

Hercule Poirot
was described by
Agatha Christie as a "detestable,
bombastic, tiresome, egocentric
little creep."

Daniel Defoe
once had a job
harvesting musk from the
anal glands of cats.

T. S. Eliot
wore pale green makeup.
Nobody knows why.

J. R. R. Tolkien and C. S. Lewis once
went to a party dressed as polar bears.
It wasn't a costume party.

If a mother polar bear fails to
double her weight during pregnancy,
the fetus is reabsorbed
into her body.

Aztec mothers
who died in childbirth
were regarded as highly as
warriors who died in battle.

The chance of two expectant
mothers with the same due date
giving birth on the same day
is 1 in 200.

Novercaphobia is
the fear of stepmothers.

Mother cats stimulate
their kittens to defecate by
licking their bottoms.

Being born in September
increases your chance of getting
into Oxford or Cambridge by 12%.

Stephen Hawking was born
on the 300th anniversary
of Galileo's death.

Emily Brontë, who wrote
Wuthering Heights, and Kate Bush,
who sang "Wuthering Heights,"
were both born on July 30,
140 years apart.

1 in 20
Twitter accounts are
nonhuman spam bots.

Even if teleportation were possible,
there is so much data in a human being
that teleporting just one person would
take 350,000 times longer
than the age of the universe.

Saturn V,
the tallest-ever space rocket,
was taller than all but one
of the trees on Earth.

Apollo 11's
fuel consumption
was seven inches
to the gallon.

The maximum length
that a fly can grow to is
two and a half inches.

During the Second World War,
people in Okinawa read at night
using light from phosphorescent
marine animals.

In the last 200 years,
the world's oceans have absorbed
more than a quarter of the
carbon dioxide released
by humans.

There are at least
a billion tons of ice
on the Moon.

(i)

People sleep
20 minutes longer on nights
when there is a full moon.

City skies are lighter
on cloudy nights than on clear nights
(even when there is a full moon)
because the clouds reflect back
the light pollution.

Moonshine alcohol is called
"Crazy Mary" in Brazil,
"Kill me quick" in Kenya, and
"Push me, I push you" in Nigeria.

If you get a zebrafish drunk,
other zebrafish will
follow it around.

Male mosquitofish
have such large penises
they can't swim straight.

The man with
the longest penis on record
is a data entry clerk
from Manhattan.

From 1994 to 2000,
Manhattan's Twins restaurant
was staffed entirely by
identical twins.

The world record
for the most people
sitting on one chair
is 1,831.

The first execution
by electric chair in 1890
took eight minutes.

While St. Lawrence was being
executed on a red-hot griddle,
he asked to be turned over as
"one side was perfectly cooked."

St. Simon and
St. James the Less
were sawed to death.

As the hands of St. Kevin
were outstretched in prayer,
a blackbird laid an egg in them,
and he stayed in that position
till it hatched.

Magpies
prefer blue items
to shiny ones.

Rats
dream about
places they want
to explore.

To stay alive,
a hummingbird needs
to eat 300 fruit flies a day.

An attempt to make
the world's biggest sandwich
in Iran failed when the crowd
ate it before it could
be measured.

There is a
renewable-energy
recruitment agency called
Earth, Wind & Hire.

One of the world's biggest
elevator manufacturers is called
Schindler's Lifts.

One of the crown jewels is called
"the Pointless Sword of Mercy"
because it has its
end cut off.

The pipe tobacco
Baby's Bottom was named
for the smoothness
of its taste.

The most popular exhibit
in the Smithsonian's modern
physics collection is
Einstein's pipe.

Darts evolved from
a game called "puff and dart,"
which was played in pubs
with a blowpipe.

During the Second World War,
Canada tested killer darts
on sheep dressed in
military uniform.

The last time an elephant
took part in battle was in 1885,
for Vietnam against France.

During the Second World War,
Japanese soldiers hid grenades inside
coconuts and used them
as weapons.

The first shot
of the First World War
was fired in Togo, West Africa.

Nigerian
email scams were
introduced to Nigeria
by the British.

When it rains heavily
in the Sumatran rainforests,
there is a corresponding drought
in East Africa, 3,700 miles away.

The Hebrew name for the film
Cloudy with a Chance of Meatballs
translates as "It's Raining Falafel."

J. M. Barrie
nearly called *Peter Pan*
"The Boy Who Hated Mothers."

J. K. Rowling's
parents met at
King's Cross station.

In 1899,
Thomas and Alice Day
named their newborn son
Time Of.

In 1896,
the 937th most popular name
for a boy in the US was
Josephine.

Linus Pauling's sister
was called Pauline.

If Napoleon's sister Pauline
got cold feet, she warmed them
in the cleavage of one of
her ladies-in-waiting.

In 1454, Philip the Good held a feast
that included a lion chained to a pillar
protecting a statue of a nude woman
who served mulled wine from
her right breast.

The earliest known feast
consisted of 71 tortoises,
roasted in their shells.

The first recorded soup
dates from 10,000 BC, the first beer
from 7,000 BC and the first tortillas
from 6,000 BC.

Sweet-and-sour sauce
was eaten in medieval Britain.

Condors
sometimes eat so much
they can't take off.

Since 1972,
Don Gorske from Wisconsin
has eaten more than
26,000 Big Macs.

McDonald's
created
bubble-gum-flavored
broccoli.

To digest baobab seeds,
chimpanzees have to eat them,
pick them out of their feces,
and then eat them again.

Dog food
is used to test toilets because
it has the same consistency
as human feces.

Because dogs aren't allowed
at Selwyn College, Cambridge,
the Master's basset hound has been
reclassified as "a very large cat."

John Adams,
second president of the US,
had a dog called Satan.

Speedy Gonzalez
had a cousin called
Slowpoke Rodriguez.

There have been Britons called
Rhoda Turtle, Jesus Devilheart,
Dick Thick, and Willy Cockhead.

The NYPD's crackdown on
illegal cockfighting in 2014 was
called "Operation Angry Birds."

Policemen in Grenada
wear their Twitter handles
on their uniforms.

As punishment for misbehavior,
policemen in Thailand have to wear
Hello Kitty armbands.

According to the
company that created her,
Hello Kitty isn't a cat.

Cats can recognize
their owners' voices but
have evolved to
ignore them.

Every year, the Bank of England's
damaged and mutilated notes service
receives claims of over $150,000
for banknotes eaten by pets.

1 in 5 Americans
trust their pet more than
their partner.

The UK spends
five times as much on pet food
as it does on baby food.

Since we domesticated dogs,
human brains have
gotten smaller.

The same part of your brain
lights up when you hear the words
"hammered the nail" as it does when
you actually hammer a nail.

At the turn of the 20th century,
animal brains were used
to thicken milk.

Donkey's milk
is the best natural substitute
for human breast milk.

London milkmaids
used to shout "mi-ow" in the streets.
It was short for "milk below."

The arrival of cats
in North America led
to the extinction of
40 species of dog.

Snake's venom
evolved from
saliva.

A boa constrictor
monitors its victim's heart,
and stops squeezing
when it stops
beating.

The first female chief
of the Cherokee Nation was called
Wilma Mankiller.

There are American politicians called
Dick Swett, Frank Shmuck,
and Butch Otter.

More Americans think
that Barack Obama is a Muslim than
accept the theory of evolution.

The area of land
seized from Native Americans
by the US since 1776 is
25 times larger than
the UK.

The most common job
in America is
truck driver.

Until 1925, drivers going east–west
in New York stopped on amber and
drove on green, but drivers going
north–south stopped on green
and drove on amber.

Since 1902, *The New York Times* has
published at least five articles
announcing the return
of the monocle.

In 1952, the Great Smog of London
was so bad that blind people led
sighted people home from
the train stations.

You can travel by train from
London to Singapore.

If you travel to Tibet
on the world's highest railway,
a doctor is always available
to give you oxygen.

The hands of the clock
on Bolivia's congressional building
move counterclockwise to encourage
people to think creatively.

Scientists have
performed brain surgery
on cockroaches.

Signs saying
"Beware of Pickpockets"
attract pickpockets.

Male kangaroos
attract females by
showing off their biceps.

Kangaroos
swim doggy-paddle.

Due to flash floods,
one of the biggest dangers
in the desert is
drowning.

Only 30%
of the Sahara desert
is sand.

The word "scruples"
comes from the Latin *scrupulus*,
a small sharp stone that got
caught in your sandal.

The most painful place
to be stung by a bee is
inside your nostril.

Most honeybees in the US
live in hives stored
on flatbed trucks.

Ants' nests
can get infested by
smaller ants.

Dragonflies can migrate
11,000 miles
a year.

Insects in New York consume
60,000 hot dogs' worth of
discarded junk food
each year.

Morbidly obese people who are
too large for hospital MRI machines
may have to get their scans
done at the zoo.

Most of the fat
lost when dieting is
exhaled as carbon dioxide.

There is more
toxic nitrogen dioxide
on London's Oxford Street
than anywhere else
in the world.

In the 14th century,
London had a higher murder rate
than any US city today.

A London bylaw of 1351
prohibited boys from playing
practical jokes on MPs.

In the 19th century,
many main roads into London
were paved with wood.

If a woodchuck could
chuck wood, it would chuck
700 pounds of wood per day.

"Limericks"
were originally ladies' gloves
made from chicken skin
or calves' fetuses.

Baby parking
is Italian for
"daycare."

Only 3% of children of
atheist parents go on to join
a religious faith, compared to 50%
if both parents are religious.

To treat his childhood asthma,
Theodore Roosevelt's doctor and
parents encouraged him
to smoke cigars.

In the 2001 UK general election, the
Official Monster Raving Loony Party
promised to reduce class sizes by
"making the children stand
closer together."

In the 2005 UK general election,
one candidate stood in 13
different constituencies.

In 19th-century US elections,
you had to cut your own
ballot paper out of
the newspaper.

The first newspaper
in English was printed
in Amsterdam.

London's first
telephone directory
didn't have any
numbers in it.

The first known genitals
belonged to jawed vertebrates
called *Microbrachius dicki*.

There are
328 people in the US
called Abcde.

Napoleon let
the sons of the fallen
in his army add the name
Napoleon to their own.

During his campaign in Egypt,
Napoleon sent the locals
64,000 pints of wine—
but only after it
had gone bad.

At a food safety conference
in Baltimore in 2014,
100 attendees got
food poisoning.

After feeding near
an M&M's factory in 2012,
French bees started producing
blue and green honey.

The giant green sea anemone
eats seabird chicks that fall
from nearby cliffs.

Most adult cats
are lactose-intolerant.

Wimbledon keeps its
tennis balls
at a temperature of
exactly 68°F.

The best time of the day
for hand-eye coordination
is 8 p.m.

On New Year's Eve 2014,
835 of the 1,000 police officers
meant to be on duty in Rome
phoned in sick.

US presidents Washington, Lincoln,
Monroe, Jackson, Grant, Garfield,
Theodore Roosevelt, and Kennedy
all suffered from malaria.

A *cyberchondriac* is someone who
scours the Internet looking for
details of their illnesses.

The computer system
of Britain's police force is called the
Home Office Large Major Enquiry System:
HOLMES for short.

A fifth of the candidates
in India's 2014 general election
faced criminal charges.

The Yakuza crime syndicate of Japan
has launched a website and theme song
to attract new members.

Butch Cassidy's first crime was
stealing a pair of jeans and a pie.
He left an IOU, but the shopkeeper
reported him anyway.

By law, all buses in
Argentina must carry the words
Las Malvinas son Argentinas:
"The Falklands are
Argentine."

The first London buses
were so slow that operators
provided free reading material.

The first mobile library
was horse-drawn.

If all the shelves
of the Library of Congress
were arranged in a straight line,
they would stretch from
Washington, DC,
to St. Louis.

The world's deepest gold mine
could hold 10 Empire State Buildings
stacked on top of each other.

The keys used to open
the Bank of England's gold vault
are three feet long.

The richest person in Asia
is Mr. Ka-shing.

When Stephen Hawking gave a lecture
in Japan, he was asked not to mention
the possible re-collapse of the
universe in case it affected
the stock market.

No one knows
who invented
Bitcoin.

Four of the six
founders of PayPal
built bombs at
school.

The surface area
of the world of *Minecraft* is
9,258,235 times larger
than that of Earth.

The opposite of
extraterrestrial is intraterrestrial:
life deep inside the Earth.

There were no
earthworms in America
anywhere north of Pennsylvania
before the Europeans arrived.

You are three times
more likely to be bitten
by Luis Suárez if you play
soccer against him than you
are to be bitten by a snake
in a year of living in Australia.

California
ground squirrels
kick sand into
snakes' faces.

The face of
the average man has
30,000 whiskers.

Roald Dahl
suffered from pogonophobia,
an extreme hatred
of beards.

Gillette's five-bladed razor
was a joke on the website *The Onion*
a year before they got round to
producing a real one.

The first-ever
mobile phone network
could handle a maximum of
three calls at the same time
in any given city.

The first-ever
YouTube video was
an 18-second clip called
"Me at the Zoo."

The single biggest expense in
the *LEGO Universe* video game was
hiring a team of moderators to
detect if anyone had built
Lego penises.

The Colorado Rapids
Major League Soccer team play
their home games at "The Dick."

The first soccer match
in Brazil had just 15 spectators:
4 family and friends and 11 tennis players
who were there by accident.

When the New York Jets
came to play in London in 2015,
they brought their own toilet paper.
The British variety was
too thin for them.

In the 1920s,
BBC radio newsreaders
always wore tuxedos,
even though no one
could see them.

The first BBC radio presenter
with a northern accent was hired in
the Second World War to make it harder
for the Germans to produce
fake news bulletins.

If Scotland became independent,
average annual rainfall in the UK
would decrease by eight inches.

Between 1901 and 1960,
every independent country in the world
had a coup d'état—except Sweden,
Switzerland, Britain, and the US.

In 1928,
Liberia's 15,000 registered voters
elected Charles King president
with a majority
of 60,000.

In 1835,
US President Andrew Jackson
beat off a would-be assassin
with his cane.

Wherever he goes,
the US president has his food cooked
by White House stewards to
ensure it is safe to eat.

In 2012,
the president of France
banned cheese from the
presidential palace.

Winston Churchill
enshrined the tea break
into law.

The Chinese
use monkeys
to pick tea.

A group of otters
is called a romp.

A group of hyenas
is called a cackle.

To deter foxes,
the actor David Tennant
urinates in his
back garden.

In the Middle Ages,
Scottish warriors used horse urine
to dye their tunics yellow.

King Harold didn't die
at the battle of Hastings
from an arrow in his eye:
he was hacked apart by
four Norman knights.

At the battle of Dybbøl in 1864,
the Prussian assault on the Danes
was accompanied by a 300-man
military orchestra playing a
specially composed march.

There were more Scots
in the army that defeated
Bonnie Prince Charlie at Culloden
than there were in his own army.

Rawgabbit
is Scots for one
who speaks confidently
on a subject about which they
know absolutely nothing.

One job application
for an air traffic controller
in the Scilly Isles
was in Braille.

It takes three million presses
to wear out a button on
an Xbox controller.

The button was invented
more than 1,000 years before
the buttonhole.

John Cage's
composition
"Organ2/ASLSP"
takes 639 years
to play.

Orangutans
like playing on iPads,
but gorillas don't.

When the iPod Shuffle
was released, it came with
a warning saying,
"Do not eat."

Apple Inc.
was founded on
April Fools' Day.

April in England,
despite its reputation,
is usually the month with
the lowest rainfall.

In April and May,
sparrows' testicles increase
a thousandfold in size.

Hippos can retract their testicles
over a foot into their body
to stop rivals from
biting them.

The longer a
narwhal's tusk,
the bigger his
testicles.

Queen Victoria
owned two
tricycles.

The first woman
to cycle round the world
learned to ride a bike
the day before
she set off.

The first riders of
the first loop-the-loop
roller coaster in Paris
were monkeys.

When the waltz
first arrived in London,
it was called an "obscene display"
best confined to "prostitutes
and adulteresses"
by *The Times*.

At times
of peak fertility,
women's voices are
higher-pitched.

Sleep-deprived
fruit flies take longer
to learn things.

Your brain cells shrink
when you're asleep.

The first person
to study sleepwalking was
Lord Byron's friend John Polidori.
His recommended cures were beatings
and the application of electricity.

Queen Elizabeth I
was wrapped in a red blanket
to cure her smallpox.

King George IV
had eight boxing champions
as his pages for his
coronation.

King Richard II's chefs
wrote a cookbook that
included a recipe for
porpoise porridge.

The Royal Mint
is a cashless workplace.

The first pair of Nike
trainers was made
in a waffle iron.

Kim Jong-un's wife
was a member of North Korea's
national cheerleading squad.

Robert Mugabe's wife Grace
received her PhD from the
University of Zimbabwe
two months after
she enrolled.

The world's largest
female-only university
is in Saudi Arabia.

Red lipstick
boosts waitresses' tips
from male customers, but not
from female ones.

Cheiloscopy
is the study of lip-prints;
they are as useful to police
as fingerprints.

The fingernails of
the middle fingers grow
faster than the others.

The toenails of
male terrapins are used to
hold onto females
during sex.

When a list of
all-time basketball greats
was assembled in 1940,
the average height
was 5'10".

By the end of her life,
Queen Victoria's bust measured
seven inches more than
her height.

Fear of heights
only begins six weeks after
a baby learns to crawl.

Maternal stress
causes more adverse effects
in male fetuses than
in female ones.

The first home pregnancy test
in the US included a vial
of sheep's blood.

Online sales
of baby equipment
peak at 4 a.m.

80% of dreams
are about normal things
like washing up or
being at work.

5.2% of men have
kissed a monster in their dreams,
3.4% have had foreplay with an animal,
and 1.7% have had sex with
an "object, plant, or rock."

Dreams happening
later in the night are
usually more positive
than earlier ones.

The Chinese
don't "sleep like a log,"
they "sleep like a
dead pig."

The man who discovered
rapid eye movement
nearly called it
"jerky eye movement."

Magic tricks
used to be called
"Hanky Panky."

Charioteers in ancient Rome
were not allowed to hamper
their opponents with
magic spells.

Early depictions of Jesus
show him with a
magic wand.

*"Kerosene lamp
bilong Jesus gone bugger-up"*
is the expression used by the
Koorie people of New South Wales
to describe solar eclipses.

(Q)

In the Senegalese version of Firefox,
a "crash" is a *hookii*, which means
"a cow falling over but
not dying."

The French
for 1960s pop music
is *yé-yé*.

The French
for "pie chart" is
un camembert.

Until the 1920s,
Camembert
was green.

In 16th-century Venice,
it was the height of fashion
for ladies to color
their nipples.

Ladyboy gangs in Thailand
apply sedatives to their nipples,
knocking out unsuspecting men who
suck them and can then be robbed
while they're asleep.

Charlie Chaplin
had sex with more than
2,000 women.

Male hedge sparrows
have sex 100 times a day,
but each time takes only
a tenth of a second.

Male honeybees die after sex;
their genitals detach from
their body with
an audible
"pop."

US slang terms for
sex in the 19th century
included "fandango de pokum,"
"buttock-stirring," and "being
amongst the parsley."

400 million years ago,
mushrooms grew
24 feet tall.

An 11-ton mushroom
found in Crystal Falls, Michigan,
was the inspiration for the annual
Humungus Fungus Festival.

Names for British fungi include
the jelly ear, the bearded tooth,
the weeping toothcrust,
the slimy earthtongue,
the fetid parachute, and
the hairy nuts disco.

The inky cap mushroom
is edible, but poisonous
if mixed with
alcohol.

Corona beer
is never drunk with
a slice of lime
in Mexico.

There is
an Irish pub
in Guantánamo Bay.

[217]

Cuban
emergency services
use sniffer
rabbits.

KitKats
in sweet-potato
flavor are available
in Japan.

Sweden has
a ski-through
McDonald's.

The US is
visited by more
missionaries than
any other country.

Medical students
in 18th-century Scotland
could pay their tuition fees
in corpses.

In 18th-century England,
"delivering a flying pasty"
was wrapping poo in paper
and throwing it over a
neighbor's wall.

Modern sewage systems use
more than 1,000 tons of water to
move each ton of solid waste.

It takes 100 times as much water
to make Coke cans and bottles
as it does to make the
Coca-Cola itself.

10% of all the water
in ancient Rome went
to the emperor.

The Roman emperor Commodus
renamed every month of the year
after himself and rechristened
Rome "Commodiana."

The Roman Empire
was only the 17th-biggest
empire in history.

Types of Roman gladiator included
essedarii, who rode chariots,
laquearii, who had lassos,
and *andabata,* who
fought blindfold.

In flight,
bats' hearts beat
1,000 times a minute.

Before they can take off,
bees have to warm up their
flight muscles.

Early aerobatic display teams
tied their biplanes together
before taking off.

"To take off
your considering cap"
was an 18th-century
euphemism for
being drunk.

The logo for the
Royal New Zealand Air Force
is the (flightless) kiwi.

The man who
invented and flew
the first airship held rehearsal
dinner parties with 10-foot-high
tables and chairs to simulate
dining in midair.

Doritos
were invented at
Disneyland.

The sports bra
was invented in the 1970s
by sewing two jockstraps
together.

Bill Lear invented both
the Learjet and the
8-track cartridge.

The selfie stick
was invented
in the 1920s.

E-cigarettes
were invented
in 1963.

The Inuit word
tawakiqutiqarpiit
means "do you have
any tobacco for sale?"

Ottoman emperor
Murad the Cruel put
25,000 people to death
for smoking.

The punishment for smoking
in 17th-century Russia
was castration.

Castration prevents
male-pattern baldness,
providing it is done before
any hair is lost.

The male-pattern baldness
of King Louis XIII meant French
aristocrats wore wigs
for 200 years.

For 200 years
after tomatoes reached Europe,
they were grown for purely
ornamental reasons.

Red tomatoes evolved
as a result of a meteorite strike
60 million years ago.

Eating a British-grown tomato
is three times as bad for the
environment as eating
one grown in Spain.

Spain has
more vineyards
than France.

Oklahoma has
more earthquakes
than California.

On August 28, 2014,
1,187 earthquakes were
recorded in Iceland—
almost one a minute.

Every public tweet
is recorded in the
Library of Congress.

Going to the library
produces as much happiness
as a $2,045 pay rise.
Going to the gym
is like losing
$1,983.

In the 18th century,
"to vowel" was to issue
an IOU after losing
at gambling.

Dostoevsky
wrote *The Gambler* to
pay off his gambling debts.

The 1950 book
How to Survive an Atomic Bomb
recommended wearing a hat
to shield you from
the atomic flash.

"Bang novel" is
the literal translation
of the Danish for
"thriller."

Napoleon wrote a
romantic novella aged 27,
when he was already a
successful general.

Before he wrote *Tarzan*,
Edgar Rice Burroughs was
a pencil-sharpener salesman.

Roald Dahl was
buried with a bottle of Burgundy,
his snooker cues, a power saw,
and some chocolate.

Bela Lugosi was
buried in the cape he wore
in the movie *Dracula*.

Leonard Nimoy's
two autobiographies are called
I Am Not Spock and
I Am Spock.

Dolly Parton
has a theme park
called Dollywood.

Mazes in Germany
are called *Irrgarten,*
or "error gardens."

Sheep in mazes
tend to turn left.

A volunteer shepherd
is called a "lookerer."

Camel spiders move
so fast they are called
"Kalahari Ferraris."

Boudoir
is French for
"pouting room."

Danish law
makes it illegal to
desecrate the flags of
foreign countries but
legal to burn the
Danish flag.

The Russian flag is
planted at the North Pole,
at the bottom of the Arctic Ocean.

Floating in the world's oceans
are 5.25 trillion pieces
of plastic.

The silverware
on the *Titanic* included
100 pairs of grape scissors,
1,000 oyster forks, and
2,000 egg spoons.

The champagne
in a 170-year-old bottle
found on the Baltic seabed was
described by wine experts as
"sometimes cheesy" with
"elements of wet hair."

[231]

In France a
"limousine liberal"
is a "caviar lefty."

In France a
"can of worms"
is a "basket of crabs."

The last public guillotining
in France took place in 1939.
The actor Christopher Lee
was there to see it.

A pig was hanged for
sacrilege in France
in 1394 for eating
a communion
wafer.

9 out of 10
onions are eaten in
the country they
were grown in.

Portugal is the
only country in the world
where all drugs
are legal.

Saudi Arabia is the
only country in the world
with no national women's
soccer team.

The only countries
in the world that don't have
paternity leave as standard
are Papua New Guinea
and the US.

Less than 1% of
the shoes sold in America
were made there.

Since 1970,
the average female shoe size
has increased from
a 4 to a 6.

Nike owns
a patent on
self-lacing trainers.

Prince Charles's valet
irons his shoelaces.

Prince Albert
commissioned a
corrugated-iron ballroom
for Balmoral Castle.

The first credit card
was made of cardboard.

Replacement eyelids
can be made from
foreskins.

Noël Coward's way
to make a perfect martini was
to fill a glass with gin and wave it
in the general direction
of Italy.

60% of the alcohol
in America is drunk by
10% of the people.

In the 18th century,
Harvard University had
three breweries
on campus.

A sperm cell
takes twice as long to mature
as Heineken lager.

Human cells contain
all the necessary genes
to make feathers.

Birds practice their songs
quietly in private before they
perform them in public.

Baby elephants
have milk tusks.

Baby turtles
call to each other while
they're still in their shells
so that they all hatch
at the same time.

The shell of
an armadillo is
so tough that bullets
bounce off it.

[237]

The largest military tank
was made by Porsche
for the Nazis.

For six weeks in 1941,
the crew of HMS *Trident* shared
their submarine with a reindeer
called Pollyanna.

After the Falklands War,
the Argentinian surrender document
was mislaid by the British
for over a year.

Until the 1990s,
Britain's nuclear weapons were
secured with bike locks.

Britons are
16 times more likely to
understand the rules of Quidditch
than the rules of croquet.

The House of Lords is the
second-biggest legislative chamber
in the world after the Chinese
National People's Congress.

The national anthem
of Ukraine is called
"Ukraine Is Not Dead Yet."

You cannot kill a sponge
with your bare hands.

The hydraulic tools
used by rescue workers to extract
people trapped under heavy objects
are called the Jaws of Life.

The word "cemetery"
is from the ancient Greek
for "dormitory."

The Latin for pizza is
placenta compressa, or
"compressed cake."

The Museum of Bread Culture
in Ulm, Germany, has a collection
of over 18,000 objects,
none of which is bread.

The Nazis celebrated Christmas
with chocolate SS men and
swastika-shaped tree lights.

Mussolini
once worked for
the British Secret Service.

Abraham Lincoln
was 6'4" tall and wore
a seven-inch hat.

President Grover Cleveland
used to urinate out of the
window of the Oval Office.

Johnny Cash
was the first American
to hear that Stalin had died.
He was an air force
radio operator.

To identify
each other in the dark,
soldiers in both world wars
put bioluminescent fungi
on their helmets.

The silent documentary
The Battle of the Somme (1916) sold
more tickets in British cinemas
than *Star Wars*.

An early title
for *Star Wars* was
"Adventures of the Starkiller."

Movie trailers
are so named because
they used to come after,
or "trail," the movie.

The trailer for
the longest-ever movie is
72 minutes long.

The oldest Girl Scout
in America was
100 years old
in 2015.

There are more Boy Scouts
in Indonesia than in the
rest of the world
combined.

The word
"hundred"
used to mean
120.

The Turkish
for "breakfast"
translates as
"before coffee."

There are 125
species of coffee plant
but we only make coffee
from six of them.

More than half
the world's mountains have
not yet been climbed.

In 2006,
volunteers removing
litter from Ben Nevis found
a piano near the summit.

Almost 1 in 5
Beatles songs mention
the weather.

On March 24, 2015,
the temperature in Antarctica was
higher than in Madrid, Malta,
and Marrakesh.

Monaco
has six times as many
millionaires per capita as
New York.

The most money you can fit
in a standard-sized briefcase
is $780,000.

19% of Americans
think they're in the
top 1% of earners.

Men think they are
much better at math
than they really are.

Women are
more efficient than men at
gathering mushrooms.

In the first edition of
the *Encyclopædia Britannica*,
the entry for "woman" read
"the female of man."

Action Man's
actual name is
Matthew Exler.

Graham Greene
once entered a competition
to parody his own writing style.
He came in second.

A nanosecond
is to a second what
a second is to
32 years.

At one per second,
counting all the brain's
synapses would take
three million years.

For 50 million years,
birds had snouts,
not beaks.

Dinosaurs
communicated
by hissing.

Female buffalo
make decisions
by voting.

John Wayne
loved wearing his Stetson
so much he had the roof
of his car raised.

Levi's jeans
were originally called
"waist overalls."

The first beach huts
were called
"bathing bungalows."

If Bilbo Baggins's Hobbit hole
were for sale in southern England,
it would be on the market
at $13 million.

If Tuvalu sold its
embassy building in Wimbledon,
it could pay off more than a
tenth of its national debt.

More than half of the world's
cash transactions are carried out
to hide something from
the authorities.

People are more likely to lie
in the afternoon than
in the morning.

The answer to a
True or False question
is most likely
to be true.

45% of people
falsely claim to have
gone skydiving.

1 in 20 people
have hallucinated
at some point
in their life.

95% of people
are immune to
leprosy.

One treatment
for strychnine poisoning
in the 19th century was
to drink melted lard.

The microbes
living in your stomach
suffer from jet lag.

More insects
are killed by cars in
the US each year than
human beings have
ever lived.

Toyota sold
18.7 million cars
from 2012 to 2014,
but had to recall
20 million.

Vespas are
banned from
the center of
Rome.

In ancient Rome,
bakers were forbidden
from mixing with
comedians.

Competitors in the
Hong Kong ultramarathon
run up and down the same
stretch of road 25 times.

The 1863 Derby
had 32 false starts,
delaying the start of the race
by over an hour.

The world record for
horse long jump is shorter
than the world record for
human long jump.

The longest word
with all its letters in
reverse alphabetical order
is "spoonfeed."

The Bodleian Library in Oxford
got its first Chinese book in 1604.
It was 80 years before they
found someone who
could read it.

To read all the books
in the British Library at
a rate of five a day would
take 80,000 years.

The autobiography
of Colonel Sanders was called
*Life as I Know It Has Been
"Finger Lickin' Good."*

The man who
first had the idea of
using microwaves to cook food
got a one-off payment of $2.

The first published version
of "Old Mother Hubbard"
was dedicated to a
Mr. Bastard.

The first monorail
was horse-drawn.

The first powered submarine
was called the *Resurgam*, meaning
"I will rise again," but it sank
almost immediately.

The first version of *Hamlet*
was called "Amleth" and has
a happy ending.

Judi Dench
first appeared on
stage at the age of five.
She played a snail.

Children grow
faster in spring.

Spring gets shorter
by about 30 seconds
every year.

Flowers
get suntans.

Ants yawn
and stretch their legs
when they wake up.

Spiders evolved
100 million years
before flies.

Ten midges
make a swarm.

More than a quarter
of the world's population
regularly eat insects.

A recent scientific study
has concluded that there are
too many scientific studies.

182 billion emails
are sent every day,
26 for every person
on the planet.

In the 1870s,
North America had
144 official time zones.

In the time it takes to say
"one hundred and thirty,"
your vocal cords
open and close
130 times.

When you're talking
to someone face-to-face,
your pupils dilate to
match theirs.

The word "huh"
is understood in all
known languages.

The word "twerk"
has been in use
since 1820.

Until AD 837,
Halloween was on
May 12.

Pancake Day was
celebrated in the 17th century by
"cock-throwing"—beating a chicken
to death with cudgels.

Until 1970,
all pubs in Ireland
closed on St. Patrick's Day.

88%
of New Year's
resolutions
fail.

Poecilonym
is a synonym
for the word
"synonym."

Lachschlaganfall is
the condition where
a person laughs so much
they fall unconscious.

In Old English,
the word "thing"
meant "a parliament."

The word "aficionado"
originally meant "a
bullfighting fan."

Cowbells
make cows feel
stressed.

The pouches
in hamsters' cheeks
go all the way back
to their hips.

Bats
get erections
in their tongues.

Snails
use mucus to
seal their shells with
a transparent "door."

Scientists
have discovered
a species of algae that
tastes like bacon.

The portable machine gun was
invented by Hiram Maxim,
who also invented the
mousetrap.

In Toronto in 2008,
mice chewed through wires in
the ceiling of an animal shelter
and killed nearly 100 cats.

In 1901,
Edith Wagner
of New York married
her Maltese cat.

Cerberus,
the name of the
three-headed dog
that guarded Hell,
is Sanskrit for
"Spot."

Dog food
is tested on
humans.

Wild boars
wash their food.

A Siberian tit can
store half a million seeds
in a single winter.

In severe solar storms,
Earth loses 100 tons of its
atmosphere into space.

The area code for space
is the same as the
one for Texas.

The number of
American teenagers who
consider themselves "very important"
increased from 12% in 1950
to 80% in 2010.

Twice as many
American schoolgirls
would rather be a celebrity's PA
than president of Harvard.

The Harvard-Yale
boat race takes place
on a river called
the Thames.

London, Ontario,
is on a river called
the Thames.

When Columbus
traveled to America,
he thought he was
sailing uphill.

The first bus in Britain
to be powered by human excrement
ran from Bristol to Bath on
the Number 2 route.

There is a river
in Nicaragua called
the Pis-Pis.

There are 10,685 beaches
in Australia.

People from
South Sudan, Palestine,
São Tomé and Príncipe, Myanmar,
or the Solomon Islands can travel
visa-free to 28 countries.
UK citizens can
visit 147.

"MEXICO CITY"
was a postal acronym in
the Second World War meaning
"May Every Kiss [X] I Can Offer
Carry Itself to You."

The number 88
is Morse code shorthand for
"love and kisses."

Morse code
was expanded in 2004 to include
._ _._. meaning "@."

Makahakahaka
is Hawaiian for
"deep-set eyeballs."

No words in
Esperanto are more than
12 letters long.

In Norway,
to change your surname to
one that fewer than 200 people have
you must ask permission from
everyone who has that name.

In Finland,
reindeers' antlers are covered with
reflective paint so drivers
can see them.

Åland is the
only region of Finland to
have a single official language.
It's Swedish.

Swiss cheese
is losing its holes.

Jamaica, Colombia, and Saint Lucia
are the only countries in the world
where your boss is more likely
to be a woman than a man.

Three times more men than women
would pretend not to notice
if a friend broke
down in tears.

Until 1964,
women in France
needed their husbands' permission to
start a business, get a passport,
or open a bank account.

The revolving door was invented
by a man who hated holding
doors open for women.

Twister was described
as "sex in a box" by
rival manufacturers who
tried to have it banned.

The meager fish
is so noisy during sex that
it gives away its location
to fishermen, who can
then catch it.

When *National Geographic*
published its first wildlife photos
in 1906, two board members
resigned in disgust.

All worm sex
takes place in
the "69" position.

The Bassian thrush
farts when feeding;
this startles worms into
revealing their location.

Pigeons
don't bob their heads if
they are walking on
a treadmill.

To prepare for
China's national day,
10,000 ceremonial pigeons have
anal security checks.

In March 2014,
an Australian python
swallowed a chihuahua and
found itself chained to a kennel.

Ernest Hemingway
hunted sharks with
a machine gun.

Nikola Tesla
hated pearls so much that he
refused to speak to women
who wore them.

Thomas Edison
made a film of
two cats boxing.

Mike Tyson
took a minute-and-a-half to
knock out Michael Spinks in 1988,
earning $221,000 per second.

Martin Luther King Jr.
got a C+ in Public
Speaking.

Bill Clinton
learned jujitsu before
meeting Yasser Arafat
in case he tried
to hug him.

Barbra Streisand
had a shopping mall
built for her exclusive use
underneath her house.

While playing
Achilles in the movie *Troy*,
Brad Pitt injured his
Achilles tendon.

Jackie, the second
Metro-Goldwyn-Mayer lion,
survived two train wrecks, an earthquake,
a boat sinking, a studio explosion, and a
plane crash in the Arizona desert.

For each lion cub that survives,
a lioness will have mated
3,000 times.

85% of male insects
engage in homosexual activity,
but often by mistake.

To flirt,
haddocks
hum.

Only 28% of people
know when they're
being flirted with.

The "Mile High Club" is defined
by *The Oxford English Dictionary* as
"an imaginary association of people."

There is a consultant urologist
at Musgrove Park hospital in
Taunton, Somerset, called
Nicholas Burns-Cox.

In hot weather,
the Eiffel Tower grows
by six inches.

Almost all kangaroos
are left-handed.

The first animals
with fingers had
seven or eight
on each hand.

Charles Darwin thought
the menstrual cycle was evidence that
early humans lived by the sea and
synchronized their lives
with the tides.

9 out of 10 chimps
look both ways when
crossing the road.

The UK's DMV has banned
the license plate VA61ANA,
but has allowed PEN15.

Until the 1960s,
women were banned from
wearing trousers in the
Houses of Parliament.

Women in 18th-century England
who remarried but didn't want to carry
their debts over to the new marriage
had to get married in the nude.

The US nude-wedding industry
is worth $440 million a year.

There are nearly
twice as many calories
in human blood
as in beer.

Ancient Sumerian beer
was as thick as porridge and was
drunk through a straw.

To shave two seconds
off the time it takes you to
eat a pie in a pie-eating competition,
drink cough syrup beforehand.

In 2015,
the president of Belarus
officially stated that
"Belarusian sausage does not
contain toilet paper."

In the 18th century,
King George I declared
all pigeon droppings to be
property of the Crown.

The Duke of Edinburgh's
pet names for the Queen include
"cabbage" and "sausage."

The world record
for the most sausages
produced in one minute
is 36.

More than
150 billion animals
are killed by humans
every year.

The number of hospital deaths
investigated by autopsy has
fallen from 40% in 1960
to less than 1% today.

Sumo wrestling referees
traditionally carry a knife
so if they make a bad decision
they can kill themselves.

Professional boxing
is banned in Cuba because
the prize money is incompatible
with Marxism.

Pigeon breeding
and skinny jeans are both
banned by ISIS.

In 2014,
396 girls born in the US
were named Isis.

Barbie and Ken
are named after the
daughter and son of the
couple who invented them.

There are more than
2,000 Americans
named Santa.

All the 126
remaining kakapos
have names.

Pelé's
first name is Edson:
he was named after
Thomas Edison.

Three-quarters of all the
boys christened in England in the
mid-13th century were named
John, Thomas, Robert,
Richard, or William.

Uranus was
originally called
George.

The surnames
of Bradley Cooper
and Michael Fassbender both
mean "barrel-maker."

Stephen King's son
is called Joe King.

Grumpy Cat
earns more than
Gwyneth Paltrow.

Mark Zuckerberg,
Carlos Slim, and Bill Gates are
each worth more in billions of dollars
than their age in years.

When John Lennon appeared on
The Old Grey Whistle Test
in 1975, he was paid in
chocolate cookies.

Hawaii consumes
more Spam than the 49 other
US states combined.

In 29 US states,
it is still legal to fire someone
for being gay.

In 1960,
Denys Tucker was fired from
his job at the Natural History Museum
because he claimed to have seen
the Loch Ness Monster.

The world's fastest robot
can run faster than
Usain Bolt.

When Usain Bolt ran the 100 meter
at the 2012 London Olympics,
his feet only touched the ground
for two seconds.

Pro snooker player Bill Werbeniuk
could only play when drunk,
so was able to offset the
cost of beer against
his income tax.

Glasgow City Council
spends $15,000 every year
removing traffic cones from
the head of a statue of the
Duke of Wellington.

State senators in Minnesota
are not allowed to make eye contact
with each other during debates.

In 2014,
Italian parliamentary barbers
had their annual salary cut from
$160,000 to $116,000 as an
austerity measure.

In 2013,
a construction company
collecting rubble to repair a road
destroyed a Mayan
pyramid.

In 1963,
George Harrison wrote
to Beatles fans asking them to
stop throwing candy at him
during concerts.

In 1953,
a new reservoir in New York
flooded the town of
Neversink.

The first flashing lights
on Broadway had an attendant
sitting on a nearby roof to
switch them on and off.

In the early days of baseball,
umpires sat behind
the home plate in
rocking chairs.

Until the late 19th century,
the age of consent in
most US states was
10 years old.

Most of the "carving"
at Mount Rushmore was
done with dynamite.

There are more pieces
of the Berlin Wall spread
around the world than
there are left in Berlin.

For 1.4 million years
there was no improvement in
the design of stone hand axes.

The ladders of the
San Francisco Fire Department
are made of wood.

There's as much iron
in 16 pints of Guinness
as there is in one pint
of orange juice.

Feeding oregano
to cows reduces their
methane emissions
by almost half.

Excited guinea pigs
perform little hops
and leaps called
"popcorning."

Airymouse
is Cornish
for "bat."

A mouse's body
grows six new hairs
for each one plucked out.

A whale's nerves are
three times more elastic
than a human's.

Sloth sex
takes under
two minutes.

Most ducks
don't quack.

Owls are
70 times less likely
to hoot when
it's raining.

The Earth's atmosphere
contains more than
15 trillion tons
of water.

Dissolving
Viagra in water
stops flowers from wilting
for up to a week.

Sweat
contains
antibiotics.

The word
"nuppence"
means "no money."

Poker player
Archie Karas turned
$50 into $40 million
between 1992 and 1994, and
lost it all in 1995.

Americans put out
$3 billion worth of food
for birds every year.

Drunk birds
slur their songs.

Swifts can sleep
on the wing.

Lisa
is Russian
for "fox."

The president
of Sinn Féin unwinds
by trampolining
naked with
his dog.

Llamas make
excellent jogging
companions.

It's illegal in
New York City
to take a selfie
with a tiger.

The scrotum water frog
of Lake Titicaca is used as
an aphrodisiac.

Pigs on Vanuatu,
develop both male
and female sex organs
and are used as currency.

Chimps in Zambia
wear blades of grass
in their left ears as a
fashion statement.

Polar bears
eat dolphins and
freeze the leftovers.

Orangutans
breast-feed their young
for eight years.

Each of an octopus's
1,600 suckers has 10,000
taste receptors.

In 2014,
scientists named
18,000 new species.

In ancient Greece,
evidence from slaves was
only accepted in court if it was
obtained by torture.

53 of the 84 warrants issued
for torture in British history were
authorized by Queen Elizabeth I.

In the reign of Queen Mary,
anyone caught living idly
for three days was
branded with
"V" for vagrant.

The Thuggees,
a 19th-century Indian gang,
killed at least a million people.
Their favorite weapon was
a handkerchief.

When the Roman emperor
Heraclius entered battle,
his soldiers would applaud to
intimidate their enemies.

Ancient Chinese warriors
showed off by
juggling before battle.

During the First World War,
women giving out white feathers to
"cowards" often did so by mistake
to soldiers who weren't in uniform.

More than a quarter
of new cars in the UK
are white.

Children on long car journeys
are more likely to grow up to be
rich and successful if they
sit in the middle seat.

The Mr. Men were
created by Roger Hargreaves
after his son asked what
a tickle looked like.

In the 1960s,
Italian shops had a service
called "the Smearing" in which they would
spread Nutella on any slice of bread
brought to them by a child.

"Ebb" and "Flow"
are two NASA satellites.

3-D printing means
that NASA can email
tools into space.

Tom Cruise
helped design
NASA's website.

James Cameron
sold his *Terminator* script
for $1.

In the 19th century,
you could be committed to an asylum
for "novel-reading."

In 1939,
novelist John Buchan
signed the declaration of war
between Germany
and Canada.

Franz Kafka
convinced his family that
Einstein's theory of relativity
would cure his TB.

People with hemorrhoids
are more than twice as likely
to read on the loo as
those who don't.

The smell of your farts
is as unique as your
fingerprints.

Eunuchs
live 15 years longer than
the average man.

The poke-me-boy tree
only grows on the
Virgin Islands.

1 in 10 Britons
describe themselves
as "very good lovers."

A third of married Britons
describe sex as
"a chore."

Sex between
two stick insects
can last for 79 days,
with the couple attached
for the whole time.

After meeting their mistresses,
ancient Egyptian husbands
chewed garlic to hide any
incriminating odors.

Smelling
a happy person's sweat can
make you happier.

Testosterone
evolved from
estrogen.

In the 16th century,
women in labor were given
"groaning" beer to drink during
and after the birth.

The Isle of Rhum
used to be called the Isle of Rum.
The "h" was added by
teetotal Victorians.

The Museum of London has
a whole drawer of codpieces that
one embarrassed Victorian curator
catalogued as "shoulder pads."

The average bra
can support the weight
of three bricks.

Paper money in
ancient China bore the inscription
"All Counterfeiters Will
Be Decapitated."

Counterfeiters
in medieval Russia were
punished by having their coins melted
and the molten metal poured
down their throats.

During the UK financial crisis of 1720,
Parliament debated a resolution that
bankers be sewn into sacks filled with
poisonous snakes and thrown
into the Thames.

All swimmers
leave traces of fecal matter
in the water.

Two people die,
somewhere on Earth,
every second.

Half of your friends
are replaced every
seven years.

A group of friends in
Washington State have
been playing a game of tag
for more than 24 years.

The largest-ever
game of musical chairs had
8,238 participants.

If you unraveled
every Slinky ever sold,
the wire would circle the Earth
more than 171 times.

The Earth's magnetic field
is 100 times weaker than
a fridge magnet.

Smaller magnets mean
children are swallowing
five times as many as
they did ten years ago.

It is impossible
to hum and whistle
at the same time.

Categories at the
Good Funeral Awards include
Cemetery of the Year, Embalmer
of the Year, and Gravedigger
of the Year.

Oxford University's
Future of Humanity Institute
puts the chances of humans
becoming extinct by 2100
at 19%.

After President Eisenhower had
a heart attack, his doctor prescribed
a course of hugs with his wife Mamie.

The Celts thought that
shooting pains in the body were
caused by being shot with
an arrow by an elf.

In China, it is bad luck
to give a clock as a gift
because "giving clock"
sounds like "going to a funeral."

A third of
British adults sleep
with a cuddly toy.

On the day he died,
Martin Luther King Jr.
had had a pillow fight.

The most popular song
played at funerals in the UK
is Monty Python's "Always Look on
the Bright Side of Life."

Don't Believe a Word of It?

*Facts are ventriloquists' dummies. Sitting
on a wise man's knee they may be made
to utter words of wisdom; elsewhere, they
say nothing, or talk nonsense.*

ALDOUS HUXLEY

For anyone wishing to verify any of the
facts in the book, this can be done online
by going to qi.com/US1234 and typing the
relevant hardcover page number into the
search box. Click on the online sources for a
wide range of background material. Please
do let us know if you have a quibble or a
correction, and add your own discoveries
via our Twitter account @qikipedia.

Acknowledgments

None of this would have been possible without the doughty QI Elves hewing the factual nuggets from the Mount of Tedium. Chief among the pickax wielders were Anne Miller, Andrew Hunter Murray, Anna Ptaszynski, Dan Schreiber, and Alex Bell.

Close behind them, panning the rich silt, were Rob Blake, Will Bowen, Stevyn Colgan, Mat Coward, Jenny Doughty, Ben Dupré, Mandy Fenton, Piers Fletcher, Molly Oldfield, Justin Pollard, Liz Townsend, and Rich Turner, with further gleanings from non-Elves Carla Bennett, Laura Critchley, Lauren Gilbert, Felicity J. Muth, James Phillips, Charlie Ptaszynski, and Florence Schechter. And, as ever, weighing the bags of fact dust and testing their quality was Our Lady of the Wheelbarrow, the editor, Sarah Lloyd.

They're all marvelous—and that's a fact.

Index

This is here to help you find your favorite bits.
Like the facts themselves, we've kept it as
simple as we can.

feasts, 106, 107

feathers, 32, 236

Fecal Matter, 42

feces, 108, 132

feet, 81, 106

Ferraris, 230

fertility, 206

FIFA, 85

Fiji, 38

films, 35, 81, 82, 105, 242, 243, 273

fingerprints, 209, 301

fingers, 6, 209, 277

Finland, 34, 52, 154, 269

fire engine, 16

firefighters, 2, 14, 174, 289

fireflies, 38

Firefox, 214

fireworks, 161

First World War, 70, 104, 137, 298

Fischer, Bobby, 73

fish, 35, 66, 124, 271, 275

flags, 230, 231

fleas, 132

Fleming, Ian, 52

flies, 97, 257

flight, 21, 22, 155

flirting, 275, 276

floods, 70, 181, 288

flowers, 292

flying pasty, delivery of, 219

food, 121, 124, 125

food poisoning, 188

food rationing, 60

footprints, 62

fossils, 62

foxes, 201, 294

France, 2, 15, 70, 73, 79, 103, 176, 214, 230, 231, 270

Frankenstein's monster, 34

Franklin, Benjamin, 7

ABOUT THE AUTHORS

John Lloyd CBE is the creator of QI
and the man who devised *The News Quiz*
and *To the Manor Born* for radio and
Not the Nine O'Clock News, *Spitting Image*,
and *Blackadder* for television.
His favorite page is 239.

John Mitchinson, QI's Director of Research,
has been both bookseller and publisher
and looked after authors as diverse as
Haruki Murakami, The Beatles, and
a woman who knitted with dog hair.
His favorite page is 195.

James Harkin, QI's Senior Researcher,
has a math and physics degree, a dark past
as an accountant for a chain of pubs, and is
nicknamed "Turbo" for his phenomenal work rate.
His favorite page is 2.